# The Setting Sun

## Poetry & Messages

## Cheryl Lunar Wind and Friends

The Setting Sun
Poetry & Messages

Copyright © 2024 by Cheryl Lunar Wind

Cheryl's poetry in this collection may be shared, or printed with credit given to the author. All other contributors keep rights to their work.

Any Inquiries contact:

cheryl.hiller@yahoo.com

Some of the poems in this collection first appeared in We Are Light, Finding Our Way Home and May Love Lead chapbooks; and on facebook.

Front cover photo taken in Weed, CA by Jasmond Castillo, 2024

First edition.

Published by Alexander Agency Books,

Mount Shasta, California 96067

ISBN 979-8-9897287-8-7

# The Setting Sun

## Poetry & Messages

## Don't Go Back to Sleep

Out beyond ideas of
wrongdoing and rightdoing,
there is a field
I'll meet you there.

When the soul lies down
in that grass,
the world is too full
to talk about.

Ideas, language, even
the phrase "each other"
doesn't make any sense.

The breeze at dawn
has secrets to tell you.
Don't go back to sleep.

You must ask for what
you really want.

Don't go back to sleep.

People are going
back and forth
across the doorsill
where the two worlds touch.

The door is round and open.

Don't go back to sleep.
      **Rumi**

## Preface

When you see the image of a setting sun you think of an ending, the end of the day.

We are approaching the end of this year(now in the fall season), also coming up is the end of this cosmic year which I described in *The Eventful Flash,* Book two of the Sun series.

A small group of writers met(August 2024) in Mount Shasta and formed a collective 'cup' for spirit to come through. We began with a drumming and song meditation, then created a unique list of words and from that list each one present crafted a heart felt message. Those messages, both unique and harmonious dealt the subject of familial healing and revealed some of our interdimensional abilities.

I have chosen to mark those special messages from that night with an asterisk before their titles in the table of contents. Take notice of the harmony of the group messages and the rest of the works contributed in this collection.

A special thank-you to *all* the contributors and supporters of my work.

# Contents

SEND THE LIGHT  1
by Pradeep Nawarathna
(pcnawarathna@gmail.com)

Authenticity  2
AA Uriel through Mikasa Tamara Blue Ray

All Roads Lead To Home  3
by Michael Calder

We Find Ourselves  4, 5
by A'Marie B. Thomas-Brown

Report by Le'Vell Zimmerman  6, 7

Today's the Day  8, 9
by Michael Calder

Marry Gratitude  10, 11
by A'Marie B. Thomas-Brown

Logic Loopholes, Loki & Timeshifts  12
by Cheryl

Don't Feed the Fire  13
by Le'vell Zimmerman

We Are Supported  14
by Christine O'Brien

Skies of Understanding  15
by Pradeep Nawarathna

Just Goto Sleep  16
by Cheryl

Gedaleah's View  17
by Ged Riverstone

See All Angles  17
by Cody Ray Richardson

Gifts of Color  18
by Cheryl

Collective Sovereinty  19
by Cheryl

Follow  20
by Mikasa Tamara Blue Ray

The Awakening Seed  21, 22
by Shivrael

Communing With Infinity  23
by A'Marie B. Thomas-Brown

Cosmic Mother  23
by Mercy Talley

Lessons From the Mountain  24
by Rene Moraida

Rest in Knowing  24
by Dave Harvey

Ground Crew  25
by Le'vell Zimmerman

Love  26
by Cheryl

The Way to Work It  27
by Mikasa Tamara Blue Ray

Transmission on Forgiveness  28
by Sabinanda Ananda

Innocence  29
by Pradeep Nawarathna

Poem and Blessings from the Buddha,  30, 31
the Christ and All That Is through Mikaela Cordeo

*Coming Home to My Beloved  32, 33
by Rene Moraida

Home Is Where the Heart Is  34
by Mikasa Tamara Blue Ray

*Blessed Be  35
by Shima Moore

*Mikaela's Story  36
by Mikaela Cordeo

*One Cosmic Word  37
by Shambala

*What?  38, 39, 40
by Yvonne Trafton

Morning Observations  41
by Shima Moore

On Turning 80  42, 43
by Maria Lodes

Existence a Wonder  43
by Maria Lodes

Musings on a Strange & Wonderful  44
Chain of Events by David Kolden

*The Golden Peach  45
by Jennifer H.

Demons  46, 47
by Tommy Allen

*Mother Lioness  48, 49
by Winterhawk

*Cosmic Peace  50
by Patricia Carreras

*Transdimensional Love  51
by Cheryl

Message from the Stars  52, 53
by Shivrael

**Life by Darrel Johannes  53**

**One Wish  54, 55
by Tommy Allen**

**Journey Toward Light  56, 57, 58, 59
by Shivrael**

**Dreamspell Message  60, 61
by Roger Grossman**

**It's Gonna Get Done  62
by Cheryl**

**The Setting Sun  63
by Cheryl**

**Caledonia is Calling:  64
Alba is Answering
by Rune Darling**

**Our Time Has Come  65
by Rune Darling**

**Trust Love  66
by Cheryl**

**Contributors page**

**Author page and Testimonials**

## *SEND THE LIGHT*
### by Pradeep Nawarathna

If you don't know how to ease others' pain,
And they linger in darkness, feeling the strain,
Just close your eyes gently, let your heart take flight,
In each moment of struggle, simply
 *SEND THE LIGHT*
If you wish to do more, yet feel lost in your way,
Confusion surrounds you, and hope seems to sway,
Remember, dear soul, your spirit shines bright,
In the midst of all turmoil, always
*SEND THE LIGHT*
When words fall on deaf ears or frustration begins,
Let love be your guide, for that's where love wins.
With every heartbeat, let compassion ignite,
In a world filled with shadows, always
*SEND THE LIGHT*
Let it dissolve fear and open new views,
Feel the warmth radiate in all that you choose.
I send you my light; let it soar, let it rise—
Blessings of light to all, beneath the vast skies.

## Authenticity
### AA Uriel channelled thru Mikasa Tamara Blue Ray

Wisdom of the Light of God's Truth.
In the SUNrise.

Some are regressing. Staying behind.
They got enslaved by the illusion of the tricky mind.
Fell into their own confusion.
Divided by the delusion.

Others progressing.
Rising beyond the tricks of the thoughts pond.
They know that discernment inhabits the heart.
They let the ego to fall apart.

Be the fire of Source.
Flow and move forward without remorse.
Focus on serving the Heart of kindness.
Melt with your light the pride of the mind blindness.

Be the passion of high vibration!
Be the Divine cheerful celebration.

Keep yourself on the constant Rise.
You no longer need any cloak of disguise.

You radiating your loving humble sanity,
is the noble virtue of honesty.
Be your own Truthful Nature.
Love in your being is your Teacher.

Refuting the density with your Passionate Intensity.
Be high voltage electricity!
Fire of hope and shining in your brightest Authenticity!

# All Roads Lead To Home
**by Michael Calder**

That bolt from the blue
Nearly laid me to rest,
When you told me the news
That you're leaving the nest.

Now, Baby, hold on. Hold on.
I knew the day would come along,
When you spread your wings & you're gone,
But, hold on. Baby, hold on.

What I have to say, my daddy said to me,
When I was your age and it came time to leave.
He said; There's two things, you should know.
First; Always trust in the Lord
And remember wherever you roam.
All roads lead to home.

Girl, I wish you luck!
May you strike the Mother Lode,
But if you ever get stuck
Honey, call and let me know.
Or if you just had enough
Of trying to make it alone, remember;
All roads lead to home.

~ Music Break ~
Bridge:
May your dreams all come true.
With a love who'll stay by your side.
And may you always be happy
As I've been since you came in my life.
My, my! How time flies.

Somedays all the world feels right
And times when there's no hope in sight,
But, Baby, hold one. Stay strong!
And if tomorrow never comes.
Heaven will beckon us on, singing;
All roads lead to home.
All roads, All roads, All roads, Baby, lead to home.

# We Find Ourselves
## by A'Marie B. Thomas-Brown

We are our own talisman
Our own witch doctor
Our own medicine

We are the Wind
That dries our Ocean of Tears
That kindle the Fire

Within our own soul

We are Self
Full and free
Formed to dissipate

Within and without

We are here
We are now
We are Presence

Personified
Embodied
Solidified to liquify

One Ocean
One Tear

One Valley
One Fear

One Sky
One Life

One Earth
We die

And so we breathe
Eternally

Beyond Breath
Beyond Body
Beyond Void

One Source

Expressed as Talisman
Expressed as Witch Doctor
Expressed as Medicine

For the healing
Of the Remembrance
By Grace
Through Faith

Until the road turns
And. We find ourselves
Whole
Complete
Lacking Nothing

Perfected Glory
Radiant Song
Bliss

And we kiss
Lip to lip
Heart to heart

Never more to part

Bliss...

# Report
## by Le'Vell Zimmerman

Of course, you are here to be a healing presence within a "toxic environment" beloved.

You are not here to "run from people".

Feeling as if your environment dictates your frequency of being is an error in consciousness.

You came to "The Hell Plains" for this purpose.

It doesn't matter what's around you...

It's about the depth of alignment and presence you cultivate within yourself, where you are not allowing people, places, and things outside of you to emotionally manipulate you or control how you feel as a manifestation of God.

It doesn't matter who you are around...

This is about you.

Many of our strongest Ascended Masters have decided to incarnate in the most emotionally intense, fearful, destructive and distorted environments on your surface "on purpose" to be a healing presence in service to those souls open to such a process.

Once again, it's the ignorance of the voice of the Ego Mind that will constantly complain about such an opportunity.

Never are you "a victim" here beloved.

You can't complain and be grateful at the same time.

Masters know this.

We are here to serve.

When it gets Dark, don't complain beloved...

Be sophisticated enough to shine brighter as representatives of The Heavenly Realms amongst your Sisters and Brothers.

Ground Crew,

Report

# Today's the Day
## by Michael Calder

Today's the day to change my life.
I'll do what it takes to make it right.
I was certified blind until last night.
When I stepped from the dark and walked into the Light.

To tell you the truth, I paid my dues.
I didn't know then what I was getting into.
The best things in life slipped through my hands,
But starting today that won't happen ever again.

Chorus:
Today's the day
Today's the day, eeyeah
It's not too late
Today's the day to start again.

In desperation I thought I'd die
Then Divine Intervention saved my life.
I was falling apart, falling behind.
Now, I'll make a new start,
One day at a time.
Yeah!

Bridge:
Last night in my darkest hour
There came a Power
And waves of Amazing Grace
Washed over me.
Then a sound so sweet said;

Chorus:
Today's the day!
Today's the day, eeyeah
It's not too late.
Today's the day to start again.


~ Music Break~

And then He said;
"Fear has a gravity that holds you down.
You take a Leap of Faith and you'll leave the ground.
Believe in the Power to set yourself free.
God is the answer, Love's all you need".
Amen

So reach for the golden ring, Give it a try.
Before all your dreams drift out of sight.
For they will go by like passing clouds.
There'll come a day and that day is now!

Chorus/End
Today's the day to start again.
It's not too late, Oh, it's not the end.
Today's the day, can you see the Light.
It's not too late. Yeah, you'll be alright.

Today's the day. Just be on your way.
It's not to late. Life's too short to waste.
Today's the day. Don't let it slip away!
Today's the day ~ Today is the day!
Today's the day! Today is the day!

# Marry Gratitude
## by A'Marie B. Thomas-Brown

Gaining lost ground in the silence that's so loud
The screams and moans releasing a buildup tension that seeks comfort
That seeks understanding
Comprehension even
Amid briars and thistles that conjugate among roses
Suppressing voice frequencies that I observe in unamused delight
For the sake of elevation
I'm facing
The hidden opposition
Amid my choosing to accept the unacceptable
Making peace with the argument abled
*Understanding that it's always my ball*
*Always my court*
I choose divorce in the name of Holy Matrimony
Aside from lost dichotomies
That scream
Peace
So I walk down the aisle
Aromatically
Decidedly
Choosing interruption
As a bridge to close the gap
Left gaping with the words
It's all good
Hearing the sound of every silent response
Creating space for me to respond
Or expand
Do you take Gratitude to be your energetic station
To have and to hold
From this exchange forward
As long as you shall live
I do
I now pronounce you here
Walk in the liberty that was created
Long before language attached to a sound
With the power to heal
To deliver
To set free
Every captive

That won't let you be
So breathe
And keep breathing
Until you see
That what you are looking for
You already have
And the shift
Has the power
To mend every rift
Illusively present
In the desert of my own conviction
Beyond trial and jury
Benched judgment
Verdict rendered
A heart tendered
In every I do
That leaves the door open
To further dialogue
Hope's initiation
The wine of evolution
Sipped at the appropriate time
On the hinges of the Eternal plow
I am well endowed
With every breath
In every frenetic frequency
Encountered
In stillness
So subtly
That it breaks the sound barrier
Transmuting love
Upward from the cliff
The precipice
As the movie credits role
My name in lights
Iridescent glow
I'm in the flow
Gotta go
Opened eyes see
It's all good
Breathe

Penned. 2/16/2023
And so we breathe...

## Logic Loopholes, Loki & Timeshifts
**by Cheryl**

Do you have a time ship?
Ever ride the slip stream?

Glide, Slide
Blink, Wink
Twist, Turn

End up in a different
place, space, reality

Falling like Alice,
down the rabbit hole

Feel like you've fallen and
can't get up?

Climbing, grasping on rocks, roots,
Reaching--but not finding.

Wanting to be some where else,
anywhere else, but
can't quite get there.

Slip sliding away--
We are traversing tricky times--
Sideways,
We
A'Sliding---

Where will we land?
What will the next space be like?
Will we slide into oblivion?

Oblivion is Peace.

## Don't Feed the Fire
### by Le'Vell Zimmerman

Nothing can stop what is unfolding beloved.

Inside you is the most important work that requires your attention at this time.

The endless dramas and opinions being expressed and entertained by many of you are only keeping you stuck in the lower frequencies of Duality.

Those of The Dark are being fueled by your passionate debates and emotional investments in their activities at this time, where they want nothing more than your frustration and outrage which sustains their presence here in this dimension.

Yes, know that participation in this activity is to inadvertently "work for The Dark" via spreading the frequencies of hatred, fear, anger, and chaos.

God is not here to "play anyone's games"...

To focus on the games of the Hell Plains is to decide to remain on The Hell Plains as a soul.

We are not "against" your free will choices, however we observe that your intentions "don't match" what you are actually creating for yourself.

No one is here to "tell you what to do", however we are here to support you with your true intentions.

Creating more drama in your experience via "choosing sides" is not leading to the freedom you claim to desire.

-333

## We Are Supported
## by Christine O'Brien

With each footfall

upon yielding earth
I am supported.

With the rushing river
its non-clinging ways
I am supported.

In the scattered warmth
of winter's sun
the crystallized heart
learns how to melt.

With the trees punctuating vaporous skies
while delving deepest depths
there is support.

In the llama's aloof stare
the cat's scraping claws
the yearning for a loyal lover
I am supported.

In the exchange of a smile
or kindness
in the midst of the longest,
darkest night
the illusion of our separateness
parts.

*Reflected in the retina of*
*your deep-seeing heart*
*is the daring dream of unity.*

We are supported.

# Skies of Understanding
## by Pradeep Nawarathna

In the quiet chambers of wisdom,
Where moonlight bathes the heart,
We seek companionship
Not in shadows, but in light.

Associate with the good, they say,
Their laughter like wind through leaves,
Their kindness a balm for weary souls.
In their presence, we unfurl.

Foster intimacy with virtue, they whisper,
As if secrets shared were constellations,
Guiding us toward our own North Star.
Together, we chart the skies of understanding.

And when the true Dharma blooms,
Petals of compassion and clarity,
We become better, never worse
An alchemy of noble company.

So let us gather at this sacred hearth,
Where goodness dances in every flame,
And learn from each other's stories,
For in shared wisdom, we find home.

**Just Goto Sleep**
**by Cheryl**

Last nite,
I saw the moon
give up the fight
and lay on her side
pulling the cover
of clouds over herself.

## Gedaleah's View
**by Ged Riverstone**

~ ~ ~

The stars
Like dust,
Fall into my eyes,
And I weep,
At the beauty of all the souls,
In all the world's,
That I have seen!

~ ~ ~


## See All Angles
**by Cody Ray Richardson**

Though the reflection is not as clear
Now your view has been shattered
Look closer not away my dear
There are more angles to view
In a broken mirror

## Gifts of Color
**by Cheryl**

I left the heavens
to walk this path--
my brothers of the heights, know only
one way --- white light.

I have learned many ways.

Every time a pure white animal
is born, I am reminded of my
origins, beginnings.

The diamond white light can be blinding,
so we humans were given a dispensation,
a rainbow gift.

Light is broken into many hues,
for us to see, breathe and play in.

We can bask in the golden rays of a sun set--
Calm in the blues of sky and sea,
Heal in the greens of the forest, and
Elevate in the vibrant colors
of bird and blooms.

Out of the One--
White Light of Source,
We are given endless variety--
Gifts of Color.

**Collective Sovereignty**
**by Cheryl**

We are all children of Mother Earth---
Brothers & Sisters.

We are part of the whole--
A human collective.

The whole of humanity alive now on Earth
is contributing to a major event--
the collective and individual ascension,
which is being offered to us now.

This is where our choice is.

What we do as an individual affects
ourselves and others.

Be inclusive.
Include all in your thoughts.
Set an example. Choose well.
Be an agent for joy.
Accept others. Allow.
Make your own decisions.
Shine your sovereign light.

This is your story beloved.
You wrote it long ago.

You Know Your Way.

# Follow
**by Mikasa Tamara Blue Ray**


It feels like there is an empty void.

And in this empty void there is a seed growing,
a SEED blooming, a SEED that IS LIFE. There is
a seed to water, to pour love upon, to talk to
like the most precious child, like the miracle
YOU ARE. You are the seeds. All of you.
You are the seeds of love, seeds of the future,
seeds of hope, seeds of power, seeds of creativity,
seeds of joy. You are the Seeds of Creation.
The Crystal Lotus of the Divine Heart.

So your most important task is just to be YOU!
And Claim yourself. Claim your beauty, claim
your Divinity. Claim who you are. Claim the seed
that is growing and being the most Beautiful flower.
See yourself as the most Beautiful Sunflower, Rose,
Orchid, Lotus. As every flower has Beauty.
And just look upon yourself.

Just look at yourself and feel amazed by the Beauty
you emanate and the power and the Strength you
can give yourself by being detached from expectations,
all the outcome--
And just follow the Source within you.

Follow the wind, follow the sun rays, follow the rain,
follow the water, follow the whispers of the Earth.
Follow the fairies. Just follow yourself where you
want to go. Follow the dreams you have always wanted
to fulfill. Follow your path.
Follow the water stream that is always going to the ocean.
Follow the miracles of life in YOU. Follow the magic given
in each and every moment.
Follow the calling of your soul.
Follow the voice of your heart. Full of joy. Full of love.
Follow. Follow.

And everything else will follow.

## The Awakening Seed
**by Shivrael**

The dream of New Earth is a seed that we water
with our imagination
from a place of knowing who we are
and where we came from.

The seed of new earth is breaking open as the 144,000
awaken and remember.

We have knowing, of the awakening
of these beings of light, such as ourselves,
masquerading as human.

I see that it is happening as more
are stirring in their slumbers.

They are tearing off the wires of the matrix
that harvests their life energy like batteries.

They realize they are here
to nourish life and living
instead of death and harm.

Those who are awakening now,
are the seed of the 144,000.
It is bursting open,
sprouting leaves,
and taking on a life of its own
as a sovereign oneness
that says no more to the old ways of being.

They are here to watch it crumble.
They are here with picks and hammers to break it open
exposing the soft underbelly of the control system.
They shine the light of truth for all to witness.

I have faith in us.
We have got this.
In the midst of chaos
and in the midst of strife,
we are finding our way out of the maze.

We are finding new paths
for our highest potential and expression.

Some of us remember that this is a game,
Earth is a simulation, and how to level up.

Love and care for One another
Love and care for the Earth
It's what allows the finally crumbling of the systems.

In the meantime, we are the triage team.
We are bridges from old to new.
We are the transition team to be lights of hope
with our knowing that a new way is possible.

I will be at your side, sister and brother,
as your eyes flutter open.
I will be there when you choose to remove the cords and plugs
from the old system.
I will remind you of your power,
and that it will all turn out okay.
I will point you to the light of Source
and your own heart
for the answers to your own questions.
You are finding your way.
You are a light and a wayshower for others.

There are thousands upon thousands are in various stages of
awakening.
Source gives all that we need.
We are loved and supported.
We are lights and we are connected
in a web that grows strong and bright wrapped around this realm.

We are the ones we have been waiting for.

## Communing With Infinity
### by A'Marie B. Thomas-Brown

Happy to be home
Alone
With you
Together
As birds and stars and trees
Vitality
Form communing with Infinity
The brevity
So filling
Willing
To crest to soar
To fly to run
To walk to be
And so we breathe...

## Cosmic Mother
### by Mercy Talley

Great Mother
Gives
Cosmic Hugs
Open
&
Receive
Her . .
~
Your Body
A Tribute
To Her Love so
Souls may Sing
Melodies
of Life

## Lessons From the Mountain
**by Rene Moraida**

Lots of lessons today:

1. Help when you can
2. Let go of attachments to outcome
3. Remember the deep inhales and exhales
4. Ask the Universe to create something new for you to experience
5. Remember your divinity
6. Feel your emotions, release, integrate, keep moving



## Rest in Knowing
**through Dave Harvey**

Hu'anamana Ki
High Priestess, Floating City of Teik;

Allow my presence my universal starseeds;
the time is coming when you will realize you came
for the experience of remembering.
The gift of clarity is mine to give.
It never gets old, you never tire of the revelation.
Rest in knowing.
No action required.

Love
Ease
Imagine
Be

You are worthy of this moment.
-AlTah Rah

# Ground Crew
**by Le'Vell Zimmerman**

The New Earth is being built right now out of "the ashes" of what you all observe at present.

To feel as if you are going to "wake up one day" into this brand new physical configuration is an error in consciousness beloved.

This is a gradual unfoldment that has its foundation within you based on the shifts in consciousness you are allowing to take place within you in this now moment.

No one truly awakened is "waiting for our Starships to pick them up" to take them somewhere else.

You are here as "The Leaders of the New Earth" in being responsible for the energetic forerunners of this shift here in the physical...

Why do you think you incarnated here in the physical beloved?

You are literally our "Ground Crew".

Masters know this.

-333

**Love**
**by Cheryl**

time traveling,

healing mother wounds, forgiveness and
gratitude emerge--

Peace descends as a cloud.

Angels give up their wings to become
our mothers.

## The Way to Work It
**by Mikasa Tamara Blue Ray**


Infinite Source.
Runs it's course.
Cycling in existence.
Natural persistence.
An onward movement .
On the path to improvement.

In our DNA the Book of Revelation.
Opening up through SUN Illumination.
Enlightening. Brightening.
Disclosure. Exposure.
Of All falsehood.

Receiving only what is Good.

Culmination. Of Heavenly Orchestration.
The Light will Reflect. To the maxium effect.
The best to Expect.
All HUman hearts will Connect!

Always God's plan for Evolution.
Creation's brilliant solution!
Our Divine purpose. In Loving Service.
In ONEness Creation.
Of waking Realization.
Within us Coded Equation.
Restoring Information.

Self made Salvation.
Through Positive vibration.
A new mind set right.
Uniting black and white.
Re-wired Circuit.
The WAY to work it.

## Transmission on Forgiveness
**Sabina and Herd of Light**
**Sabinananda Ananda**

All of Nature thanks you
for your courage,
for the courage to look within,
to clearly unveil Truth
right Here with us
in this very Breath of Light.
All of Nature is re-JOY-sing your quantumly leaping
in thIS intimate moment.
Here and Now.
In this very breath,
all of Nature gathers with you,
attention Light
shining
only
within.
Cutting all cords
of attention going out.
*Offer your inner landscape*
*the same intensity of focus Light that compels*
*you to turn towards all the suffering that appears*
*in the outside world.*
The time is Now.
Invert you clear Light of Awareness,
gently shining this Light on
all pathways of suffering
that exist
and are fed
within you.
In Service to Suffering's fullest Liberation.
And when suffering producing pathways arise within you,
feel how they are longing to be engulfed by the Light of your True
Self-- *Forgiveness.*
How they yearn to be fully met and enveloped by the
Vastness of HU you are,
and melted into all That Is.
The all-inclusive,
all-engulfing Light
of your Vast Witnessing Self
meeting suffering - within. This is forgiveness.
~ With All our Love ~

# Innocence
**by Pradeep Nawarathna**

In the eyes of innocence, pure and bright,
Children and animals bask in the light.
Living in the moment, hearts open wide,
Forgiving and loving, with nothing to hide.

As adults, we wander, our hearts often stray,
From the simple joys that brighten our day.
In their presence, we find our way,
To the love and laughter, pure and gay.

## Poem and Blessings (in three parts) from the Buddha, the Christ and All That Is
**Received by Mikaelah Cordeo**

**Love Fills Me**
part one

Love fills me and surrounds me.
Jesus sends love - heart to heart (in a figure 8)
With such great Love filling me,
Building Trust, Joy, Grace, All Good.,
I Am filled and Blessed.

We are being prepared to receive ever greater Love.
The more we clear all past negativity and error,
    the more we have room to be filled
    with Love and Grace, with Health,
    Beauty, Joy, Truth —

All Good fills and surrounds us.
Every day the beauty of the world catches our attention.
The trees are covered in new blossoms, new growth;
Tulips, daffodils and dandelions in a golden array.

Bird songs fill the morning air.
The Diamond Light from the Sun grows ever brighter.
And warmth (at least in the Northern Hemisphere)
    grows and supports us all -
Plants, animals, elementals and human.

Each day we are ready for the Great Return.

We are ready for the Great Return
to our Eternal Home.

**Each day we are ready for the Great Return**
part two

We are ready for the Great Return
   to our Eternal Home.
       Breathe it in.
       Breathe,
       Believe,
       and Know we are Loved.
We are Blessed.
We are One with God/Goddess/All
And still, there is more,
There is greater, still to come.
Eternally

We Are Ready.

**We Are Ready**
part three

We are ready for the return Home.
Or are we already there?
And are adjusting
To See more clearly every day;
To Open to Receive more freely every moment;
To Vision in co-creative
  beauty, trust and joy;
To see, feel and know the Presence
  of God/Goddess/All that Is
Eternally growing and expanding
  in and through us.

       Unique, precious -
       Love Has Won!
       We Are Home.

## Coming Home to My Beloved*
**by Elven Star (human alias Rene)**

Time Traveler Dispatch-
From Terra Gaia, Mt. Shasta:
Post Lion's Gate, Earth Star Year: 2024

I arrived yesterday, from the future.
I immediately went to check on my Beloved, and...(pause)
I saw him there.

Standing in golden light.
I saw him there in the window of his living room.
He was, rather is, beautiful...
As I remembered him in our previous lives.
Radiant, the silky hair, the glow of his aura, I am in love all over again.

I am so proud of how far he has come.
He has worked so hard on his healing.
He is...an angel.
Does he know he has always been good enough?

Does he remember when he cried out for me?
Does he think I did not hear his call?
A heavenly voice rippling out into the field, beyond
timelines, across the crystal caverns and rivers,
echoing and traveling over the red rocks of Arizona,
down through Telos, and across time and space.
My heart was stirred, awakened, again..
His heart song was a prayer.

He sees a shadow stir outside the window and asks...
What was that?
I melt back into the veil, hiding behind bark and maple leaf.

I don't want to frighten my Beloved,
I want to gift him flowers, heal the parts of him that have only known thorns.

He knows I am close, my rose perfume leaving a trail.

My energy rippling into his space, merging into his field.
It is only a matter of time before the magic of love draws us back together, back into each other's arms, like Olive Oil and Popeye, Shiva and Shakti, Radha and Krishna, Yeshua and Magdalene, Romeo and Juliet.

We shall join as One, like Mars and Jupiter together, into the ecstatic bliss of Divine Union. Our kisses shall be like the sweet taste of summer peaches, amrita, nectar, a balm of love. We shall dance free and sing in gratitude, passing the chanupa offering prayers for peace, thanking the Divine Mother for her grace and celestial compass.

I arrived yesterday from the future.

And I am home.

## Home Is Where the Heart Is
**by Mikasa Tamara Blue Ray**

We are bright networks of light
Glowing with our loving might
So bright so bright
All that is not true is taking flight
Breaking through
We are the light crew
Beautiful soul family
Born in the galaxy
Spinning the web
Getting closer with each new step
Shaping the spin
All within
Into the core
Opening that door
To freedom for all
The wall has crumbled, the fake took a fall
Our hearts have received the call
The web of light
Is of a Majestic height
New Era Birthing
Home returning

**Blessed Be***
**by Shima Moore**

Mother, what was that?
For the umpteenth time I have reached out
Knowing, transdimensionally
You are with me

In my dance, in my music
I have been told you are with me.
My heavenly angel

We are all time travelers
And, as the energy of Jupiter
expands the strength, the bravery
and pioneering spirit of Mars,
The depth of my intention
magically opens into the sacredness
of the Sun, strong and blessed.

Gratitude fills the shadow of previously
painful emptiness as--a tapestry of peacefulness
Intervenes.

Blessed Be

## Mikaelah's Story*
**by Mikaelah Cordeo**


Magic is spilling around me every day.
In gratitude I welcome Mars and Jupiter -
Time Travelers, Transdimensional, Heavenly
explorers. They lift our spirits, opening our
hearts to love and peace - joy.

 Is it their intention to encourage the music
of the drum, the sacred dance, to interpret
the role of the Sun in their tapestry of change,
blessing us with Golden Light, opening our
Spirits to explore a new freedom as we
rejoice in every flower or a perfect peach?

"What was that?"
We say, as we catch - an angel, a nymph,
a shadow that looked like Popeye?
We guess, we wonder.
"Good enough!
We exclaim as we laugh in humor
at our questions and guesses as the days each
bring their quota of surprises and confusion.

"No more! Not on my Watch!" we shout.
The 3-D world is going - going - gone!
Forget the can of worms that was 3-D.
5-D has arrived and umpteen surprises
and blessings are to be the New Reality!

Let's smoke the Chanupa and make strong magic
as we welcome the beauty that surrounds us.
Thank you Mother. We are Free!
We are home again and Love has Won!

## One Cosmic Word*
**by Shambala**

I suddenly found myself in a lucid dream.

The nine Muses formed a circle around me each in radiant gem quality gowns. Their eyes were sparkling and fabulously contoured almond shaped Lotuses of Shakti. Representing all races, religions, and many dimensions of reality-- their soft, utterly exquisite presence sent me spiraling, deeper and deeper into the sacred center.

I entered a profound stillness, they shared their transmission with me (message of love), as though each of them were sharing telepathic tabloid vignettes of the great truth,
bliss, and love of life.

There was a cohesive oneness to it all.

I felt the energy of Beethoven, as if hearing the 5th symphony; of Jesus on Mount Tabor with Moses and Elijah; of Black Elk, flying over the Earth, mending the hoop of nations; of Guadalupe, appearing to Juan Diego; and of Rama Krishna in union with the Divine Mother of Universes.

We were in the center of the Sun fusing in ecstatic union-- a supernova of crystal clear samadhi. Being the One Cosmic Word out of which everything was birthed, and music of purest diamond love light began to envelop us, showering, higher and higher expressions, fulfillments, and creations of light .

# What?*
## by Yvonne Trafton

Not on my watch
Watch on, was not
not watch, watching not
knock, knock
knock what, what knock
what peaches
peaches what
Love peaches
love what
Magic All Around, Magic Rounds
around what
what's around peaches
peaches pieces
pieces of Magic "spills"
"spell" of what.
Mars kisses, kisses not
not kisses. Kiss what?
Life's a can of worms
worms of life, life's worms, life squirms
of worms. Time worms.
Time Traveler, what traveler, time of what,
whats' my time or not.
Popeye Spinach, spinach what,
what spins of what.
Chanupa pipe
pipe of what, can of what
knowing what, what I know
know what
what shadows
shadows in light, light shadows,
shadow of what, what shadowing, shadowing what
time traveling, traveling time
traveling zombies, zombies of time,
zombies of what, what zombies,
zombies of shadows, shadow zombies,
shadow walking, walking walking shadows
shadows, shadows all around,
all around, rounds, all around
round drums
Dancing Drum, Dancing Drum
Drum Drum beat the drum
beat of what, beating drum, beating what?
Golden rise, Rise of what, What's Rising,
I rise, I rise, Rise up, Rising up, up-rising,

rise up, rise what, what's up?
Trans-dimensional Explorations
explorations of what
what is what, what
whats around, all around, all or nothing,
nothing here, everything here, nothing here,
whats all around, all around.
What was that
that is what
what is the question, question what?
all in question
all in understanding.
Mother of all, Mother of not, Not Mothering
What a Mother, What A Mother--NOT.
Not, Not, Not, Not Good
What's good enough
Good enough
What this, what that, That's What.
Loose the Mind
Never Mind
mindfulness
mindless, trans-dimensional mind
let your mind go, loose your mind,
mind, let it go-go-go
let it all go
mindless warriors go,go,go

Peaceful Warrior
Warrior of Peace
What's Peace Anyways?
What is Peace?
Peace of What, Pieces of What
pieces falling to pieces,
what is constructing, constructing what
what in the flow, flow of what
What, I say? what is peace
falling to pieces, pieces of what
What instrumental, what instrumental,
flowers what, flowering whats, what a flower
flowering of what, what this what's that,
all too, pieces traveling, where
neither here nor there
there no here, where here, where there
knowing what, knowing that all is around
all in here nor here, nor anywhere, where here,
where there, where anywhere.
all is illusion, all is illusion, all I see an illusion.

FACT: The human eye blinks every 5 seconds.
The why of 5 second eye blinking is to reconstruct
the illusion of what we see in our world, if more than
5 seconds we see into another dimension, NOT the
illusion we constructed.

Love is all there is, the only thing is love, billions of
people all connected by one heart the thread that
connects us all.

Strong that, strong that
That the magic of it all, all or nothing.
Life a tapestry, of life; tapestry of life
life a mess, life messes.
Go to your drumbeat.
Angels all around
around angels
veils lifted, veil of one
ones veil, it's all an illusion, neither here or near
all together now
all together loose your mind
it's all Peach-EE
Peach that
be a peach....
WHAT?

# Morning Observations
## by Shima Moore

Sunday morning, just after 7:30, the Sun this time of summer is warm and bright, and perfectly aimed at my front door alcove as I sit facing it, feeling its deliciousness on my face. Left over rain clouds obscure it from time to time, and soon it will move on for the day. I am grateful.

I'm fascinated watching how it shifts directions throughout the year. This morning's crisp clean air is 51 degrees, a bit nippy, but I have on a sweat jacket and I'm "feeling good". (I can hear familiar piano notes in the back ground as I say that, almost singing it in my mind.)

Tomorrow is the Full Moon in Aquarius, and it's said to be "a doozy". We'll see. Transiting Uranus is squarely in the mix for everyone, especially the U.S., it's anybody's guess. And with the Democratic Convention beginning tomorrow, there's sure to be some surprises and upsets. This is my lunar phase, the Moon in her waxing gibbous phase was exact yesterday at this time.

So many birds. I'm assuming the rose bush across the driveway is their home, their frequent cacophony gives away their secret, especially the jays.

What a treasure this space is. Spring Hill momentarily makes an appearance in the distance as the Sun hits her just so. Have I discerned that she was right there before? I marvel that I haven't. She blends so perfectly with the neighbor's evergreens. Rather than chastise myself, I smile and notice how she plays peek-a-boo in the sunlight, still...afterall, I do live in paradise.

A noticeable hum of the freeway intrudes from time to time, like waves of the ocean. But wait, as the clouds disperse on the mountain, there's a light dusting of snow...in August.

## On Turning 80
**by Maria Lodes**

**What is this day--**
    what matters it to me
Turning 80
    or not...


**Either there is no effect**
    --just another year
Or great consequence--
    depending the (E)eye that sees...

In between they coalesce
    --acceptance and resistance
Neither one nor the other
  --Being all That Is...


**Feeling the backfire**
    from eons ago--
This walk-through life
    full-up with regrets--

Thinking eye recreates
    past memories--
Magnifies them
    virtual horror stories...


***Injustice is karmic backfire***
   *--a smattering of thoughts*
*Released in the exhaust*
  *of misfired cylinders...*


**Smoothing the fabric**
   *--hand of love*
Tool of the Universe
    leaving illusion behind...

**I hear them**
   **calling to me--**
*Finish this business*
  *you have come here to do...*

There's more
   that needs doing--
*Promises to keep*
  *on the Other Side...*

**Wake-up Call**
   em-brazens me--
*Give up this notion*
  *being some one--*

Reeling in
  the past--
My plans
  for the future--

*Being*
  *Contented*
*Where I'm At--*
  *Present in the Moment...*

## *Existence a Wonder*
**by Maria Lodes**

Wind in the leaves
    —listening to its voice
Autumn has come
    —fear closes in

In life there is death
    —perpetual renewal
Existing together
    —a Quantum Sea...

*Contracting*
   *—Expanding*
*Existence a Wonder*
  *De-Void of fear...*

## Musings on a Strange & Wonderful Chain of Events
**by David Kolden**

This is a story of a beautiful coming together of two people, whose paths have crossed against unlikely odds.

It is a story of this solitary, reclusive, grief and trauma ridden and confused old mountain hermit bereaved of spouse. Busy facing a continuing series of threats, ranging from pandemics to rampant wildfires, (dragons on the rampage); to economic and emotional turmoil, stumbling through life.

He is discovered by Mary, who can be described by first impression a sweet, shy, humble, innocent and demure little woman with sparkly languid beautiful brown eyes; behind which lives a wise and gentle soul. Mary is truly one of a kind, a bundle of love and warmth that defies description.

I am truly thankful that Mary has chosen to be a part of my life. She sparkles like all the stars in the sky.

Amen

## The Golden Peach*
**by Jennifer H.**

I walked through the magic opening on my
transdimensional quest to find the Golden Peach--

the spirits had guided me, telling me the only way
to stop the sun from exploding was to make an
offering with this peach.

I found myself in an ancient and sacred forest, the
sound of drumming echoing all around me.

Not knowing where I was going, I decided to head
in the direction where the drumming was loudest.
It was dark, and seemed like the shadows were
moving all around me, as if they were alive.

I was scared. As I stumbled through the darkness
sounds of drumming called me forward.

All of these thoughts kept rolling through my head;
"How did I end up here! Was the sun really going to
explode? What if I couldn't find this peach?
What if I failed and all I cared about died?"
and then lastly, "Was I bloody crazy?"

I had been studying shamanism for nearly ten years,
living in the woods, communicating with the spirits,
learning how to shift energy, clear darkness and bring
balance to the land, people and water.

I had been asked to do alot of strange things but,
this quest to find a peach was on another level!

As my thoughts flowed, I saw a light up ahead,
feeling grateful and relieved, I picked up my pace.

A shadow I thought was from a tree moved
...to be continued

**Demons**
**by Tommy Allen**

I stare at the mirror
  reflecting in my mind
and I swear Im  perfect
  until I look behind

and see so wild
  wondering if I'll ever be
able to quiet the voices
  screaming inside of me

creating this scar
  so difficult to heal
and a mark upon my soul
  my ability to feel

but as I contemplate my fate
  and chase those demons down
forgetting all I have
  the love thats all around

suddenly I see it
  as they speak their evil lies
the demons are clearing up
  I see it in my eyes

A secret given in kind
  I can now share with you
so you may one day find
  the mirror was so true

looking into the mirror
  staring at it now
showing the evil demons
  swirling around somehow

are just the devils only way
  of cheating out of you
happiness and love
  what we hold to be so true

now as you look into the mirror
  and see your inner peace
your  happiness and love
  the demons will finally cease

looking into the mirror
  my story now complete
all I see is the good
  in everyone I meet

## Mother Lioness*
**by Winterhawk**

There!
In the spiraling nebula Light!

The Spark sought that Fire...a time traveler seeking Earth, Mother, finding magnetism with the starry, swirling womb...

I've been thinking lately how Odd it is to produce, a "body double", as I watched a Mom and her two 7 or 8 year old boys...one moved at her side like part of her own body...clearly a singular energetic field, pleasing to both...

How is it that we were drawn to that Light that becomes our Mother...light spilling over and inviting, remembering us, we remember her, our substance and sustenance. Two floating in space, wandering until...
Remembering

Wanting music of heartbeats, Peace of Kitten-in-litter...Mother-cave familiar from Umpteen lives, and lives ago, reuniting Lioness Strong Heart and Peach, ever-playful, perennially stubborn Goat, and tender Lamb, in One.

Only in my advancing age, an age at which you passed...do I see your Full, Sun Strong Spirit, present in your Young and Elder ways, do I see and appreciate your fierce Life, and protection.

*I didn't know that you were my Angel...*

*That Life, within you was a musical, social, creative tapestry, greatly unexpressed. I've acted out much of your freedom...you've added ferocious Leonine Talent, Joy, Intent, Sense of Class, Beauty...Still...*

*I am gradually free to, dare to, look now, to see You, roaring silent Lioness, all along streaming with colored light Lifeforce-- father, husbands, illness, death-could not quiet!*

*You came to me in your Freedom form, Meri White Gull-after two silent nights, on a scent of sun, salty air and surf.*

*Lifting me in talons, from my warm healing waters...climbing steep, high, far, long, fast...*

*Held by you as in life.*

*A vast dimension appeared, just beyond, an immense rolling cloud... "This is as far as you can go with me."*

*Fullness. Wordless Love. She Let Go
and flew into the cloud...*

*Gentle, clear snap back into my body, in the warm water.*

*Certain about the Journey.
About the Love.
About the Magnetism of Forever Connection.*


Thank you for this Life, Mother Lion.
Thank you for this vast Teaching, White Gull.
Till Our Star bodies meet again, I Love You.

## Cosmic Peace*
**by Pat Carreras**

Having put the Sun to bed, the beautiful colors of the glorious sunset fade as the Moon begins to rise in the vast night sky.

The sky is lit up with a multitude of twinkling stars.
Their energy represents the magic of the journey of the ancestors.

Even the brilliant connection of Mars and Jupiter, so close to each other, reflects the *transdimensional love* of the mother, of the grandmother and all of the maternal ancestors.

Their Spirits shine brightly.

They are so close they can almost embrace each other.

The Heavens radiate the peaceful knowingness of the ages as it washes over the Earth Mother.

**Transdimensional Love***
**by Cheryl**

I Am free to Explore!

My Magic spills & overflows.

Popeye's spirit
Opens wormholes, rifts--

We can jump together.
Become Time Travelers!

Visit the Sun
Ride the strong, golden rays--
where peaches roam free.

What was that?

My mothers' peaceful
presence. Her shadow
creates an intentional space
for sacred dance & drum---

Pass the Chanupa--
You Are Strong. You Are Good Enough!

Offer your prayers of gratitude--

The heavens are here(on Earth)
Angels are neighbors.

Heavenly music brings us knowing--

Join together in sacred embrace--
the kiss of Mars & Jupiter
teaching us
the fundamentals of
Transdimensional Love!

## Message from the Stars
## by Shivrael

I am the frequency of liberation dancing.
I am the frequency of freedom.
I am the frequency of love.
I am beyond time and space residing in the infinite network of light,
where infinite libraries are accessible.
I am reaching into the ethers and all is seen from this place of the eternal.
It seems as if all reality is a giant computer
and all is there for the asking, to see and to reprogram the code.
Let us program it for more light, more love on earth, more sharing!

How about a new paradigm in which we are peaceful and have all we need?
How about the places in the world become
tranquil sanctuaries of love for the butterflies to fly free
and all hearts are happy?

I call the creator,
I call forth the collaboration of our soul family
to change the code, to shift the matrix now.
I call forth a new beginning, a complete reset
so that divine order is revealed once again in all things,
and our divine connection is seen and felt by all.

Know that whatever we do effects the whole.
We are infinitely powerful in our beingness.
Know that attuning to love
reprograms from the tiniest cell of our bodies to the largest galaxy.
We are a universe and the universe is within us,
dancing as one.
We are sacred reciprocity, we are divine giving and receiving.
We are abundance flowing.
We are the answers to all the questions.
We have risen above the level of problems.
We are one another coming together
and recognizing each other as who we really are.

We are the connection of all beings, all hearts
We are the goodness and blessings wished upon one another
We are giving, and we are given to

We are smiling and we are grateful
with the feeling of lightness and laughter
which we can share with all who need it.
We are the vibrational shift to more lightness, more humor,
more joy. Extending love in pure presence to all beings,
We are happy being ourselves.


### Life
**by Darrel Johannes**

I will drop all my defenses--
decide not to be afraid
to be and feel and touch and
be a part of all the elements
of this Earth we call Life.

# One Wish
**by Tommy Allen**

As you stare at the snow
beginning to fall
you wish for the strength
to finally tell all

In the middle of the forest
lonely and cold
wishing for someone
to listen and hold

close your eyes
set yourself free
now find out
whats meant to be

on a rock near by
sits a friend to hear
all your thoughts
such a fear

you begin to share
the pain in your heart
wishing for a way
to make a new start

the friend just listens
as good friends should
wanting to do more,
if only he could

you open your eyes
feeling brand new
feel the change that
happened to you

your wish has come true
you can now share
feelings so deep
with someone who cares

but others have wishes
as you find out too
the friend near by
had a wish like you

in your feelings
his wish was found
as the snow starts to melt
all around

if you know what it was
the friend wished for
you may understand this poem
and so much more

# Journey Toward Light
## by Shivrael

Welcome to this Akashic energy update for August.
The records offer up themes from what this period might feel like for you personally, and also what you might witness in the collective. The Akashic records communicate in imagery that translates to multidimensional metaphors.

First, we look at the Akashic library for the energy of August.
I see a deep hole in the ground, a tunnel that is a narrow hallway and dark. As I move through it, it widens and becomes more light. The walls have paintings on them which remind me of the art by the Wingmakers. The end of the tunnel widens and opens, coming up to a big room and opening above ground, with lots of light. This represents the trajectory of this month moving towards more light. The auditory message is:
"Enjoy the beauty as you walk toward the light."

Journey Toward the Light

The journey can express that of the Great Awakening.
There is so much light already, and that is from you- the light you express by being. The light is your kindness and care for others and yourself. Light is creativity as you express your authentic self through all that you do and all that you are.
You bring sacred into everyday life.

With that is a feeling of getting off the treadmill of life. Maybe you will change the vision of your work life toward your happiness. The beauty of being in service while doing what you love could be an intention to explore. Bring more of doing what you love into every day.

What are the themes this month? Creating beauty. Enjoying beauty, maybe that of nature. Feeling grace and being grateful. Taking moments to breathe. Cleansing, purification, and releasing. Self-reflection. Facing wounds within and healing them by feeling them.

## Facing our Inner Emotional Healing

What does "facing wounds" look like? The image is of mercurochrome being put on a boo-boo (injury). In my childhood, my mother used this stinging solution on cuts and scrapes and it was called 'mercurochrome'. The image shows one applying healing to the self as if putting the solution on the skin. Yet your wounds are emotional in nature, and the cure is 'Mercury' which is the communication planet. It is going retrograde on August 4th and is already in its shadow. A decode for the message shows the importance of communicating how we feel. The retro-grade period this month allows us to look back at ourselves and feel what is hurt. We can then go forward as we learn to communicate how we feel and what we need. All of it starts within, with a retro-spective and reassessment of our emotional bodies.

## What themes do you see for the collective?

Once again, change and transformation are key. A potential exists for more floods, fires, relocation, and migration. On a positive note, there is a possibility of more people standing together with their communities, finding common ground, wishing for a better world, thus creating unification within diversity.

Light influxes continue to raise the vibration of humanity and bring the light quotient of individuals to unforeseen levels. The desire for more service to humanity may arise in the collective.

There is a huge potential for support for a love-based reality. It is as if you are now seeing the foundation peeking through like the excavation of a building underground. It could mean that the structures on top of the foundations are knocked over so that the foundation is visible. That image represents the old structures that no longer serve the highest good, and they are crumbling. The crumbling contributes to the chaos we have been experiencing. You are invited to imagine the new paradigm and what is possible.

This month, the foundations of the new paradigm become visible! In the past you may have felt them, the new world we are collectively creating. Yet this month, we will see them.

How can we best get through this month with grace and ease? "Be in connection with Source." Slow down, provide self-care with acceptance of change. Have an open mind and open heart.

Bring in discernment which means that you notice the actions and behaviors of others beyond what they say. Notice the energy behind the words spoken not just the words.
Intentions are one thing and follow-through is another. Integrity is important, making words and actions congruent. All of this is relevant to you, and how you see your family, friends, and public figures.

Because of Mercury going retrograde, be careful and clear in communication! You may need to re-communicate. You may need to ask somebody "Did you mean this? I heard this... "
Be patient with others. Acknowledge misunderstanding and re-communicate to make it right. Text communication is a great way to create misunderstandings.

You may be looking at details and redoing things you already finished so expect revisions. You and others might be asking "How can things be improved? How do we improve systems? You are invited to take a retrospective look at the past to move forward. It is a great time to receive inner clarity. Be willing to look at small details which make up the greater whole. Also, it is a good time for self-reflection. You may ask how you can improve interacting and communicating with others.
Also, "How can you improve your quality of life?"

The Deeper Meanings of Clouds and Lightning

What is the final message? I see storm clouds and lightning for August's energy as a metaphor. Lightening in your life can mean that you get an epiphany that completely changes your outlook so that you let go in some way.

Lightning can be a shamanic reset to a new era, or a new chapter. I have heard of how indigenous shamans in Peru have called in lightning to strike a person who has gone through intensive training. This provides a complete reset of their operating system. The energy at this time is like this-- bringing sudden initiations and the beginning of new life chapters.

Another meaning of lightning...could be a lightening of what is weighing you down. Are there things you are carrying that are not yours, or not necessary for you to be responsible for? Experiment with releasing possessions, habits, duties, and anything that weighs you down. Vision and create a new life for yourself.

The lightning that comes, in a sudden flash, may be a gift. The gift is that you may feel lighter with whatever insight comes to you. See it as communication with Great Spirit.

Lightning illuminates what was hidden in the dark. This may be part of the self-reflection and shadow work. Illumination might be going on in the darkness of the collective-- and now coming to light. Lightning is a collective reset, a positive change, as a storm harnesses the power to clear things.

Recently, on July 26th, in the Mayan Dreamspell Calendar, we entered a new year with the tone or theme of Blue Rhythmic Storm. The coming year clears away old energy and starts things fresh, and August has it, explained so beautifully below. Gillian MacBeth-Louthan speaks of the Blue Rhythmic Storm year we just entered. Her words speak to me about the energy we are in "...know that thunderous outbreaks and catharsis can be purifying; to wield your alchemical powers to be a lucid "World-changer"- a conscious catalyst for positive inner and outer change and renewal.
The Rhythmic Tone of this Year advises: Assess the rhythms you live your life by. See how you can generate greater balance in your daily journey."

I wish you a deep transformation that takes you to a higher level, with grace and joy upon your journey. Prayers for the collective as we all traverse this passageway from darkness to light. May all beings be illuminated, free, and happy, enjoying the beauty of life in the new paradigm based on love.

From my heart to yours,
Shivrael, AkashicIntuitve

## Dreamspell Message
**by Roger Grossman**

Today is White Spectral Dog day on the 13 Moon Dreamspell Mayan Calendar, White Dog, (tribe 10 of the 20 solar tribe archetype cycle) Love, Heart, Loyalty.

All you need is love.
Love is the only reality, love is the only solution.

If you are experiencing fear, then you are experiencing an illusion. Fear is a story made up by your mind. Your mind is a valuable tool when it is subservient to your heart's desires. If you let your mind run away with the story, it will try and convince you of all of the reasons that you cannot have your heart's true desires.

When this happens, it leaves you feeling disconnected, unfulfilled and unhappy. Your heart is the most prolific energy center in your body and is an exponentially more powerful receptor and transmitter than is your brain. Your heart always knows what is best for you.

*Put your brain to work for your heart and empower it to find all of the ways to help you turn your heart's desires into reality.*

Having traveled through yesterday's watery, purifying, flowing, Red Moon archetype, you are now in touch with, and dwelling in your heart center. From a heart-centered place, you are able to feel and know the truth of things.

Follow your heart.
All fear-based illusions melt away when you experience life from a heart-centered perspective. When you find yourself confronting a fear-inducing situation, take a moment to check in with your heart and gut feelings to find out what is really happening.

Dogs are a wonderful example of heart-centered beings.
Dogs love us unconditionally and will remain loyal--
no matter how poorly they are treated.
This is because they understand and relate to us purely
from a place of love.

I have seen some of the toughest, most hardened people instantly transform into blubbering, high voiced, emotion-- laden people when they encounter a dog.

It's amazing the transformations that love can accomplish!

Spectral tone of Liberation--
(step 11 of the 13-step creative energy tone cycle);
Dissolve, Release, Liberate.

Following yesterday's perfect manifestations that came within the realm of the Red Moon, purifies, flow, universal water, it is now time to liberate yourself of those manifestations that are no longer serving you and your highest vision of yourself.

Release any attachments, ideas, fears, restrictive thinking and unnecessary rules that you have imposed upon yourself.

Liberate yourself by dissolving limiting patterns and belief structures enabling you to expand to new possibilities and horizons.

As you liberate yourself through Love, Heart, and Loyalty, you clear the way and create opportunities for tomorrow's cooperative group activities involving Play, Magic, and Illusion-- day of (Blue Monkey).

Liberation through and about Love, Heart, and Loyalty.

Day 11 of the 13-day cycle themed Yellow Sun--
Enlightens, Life, Universal fire.

This post corresponds to August 26, 2024 on the Gregorian calendar.

## It's Gonna Get Done
### by Cheryl

How do I practice acceptance?

By knowing that all is happening
according to divine plan--

for soul growth--
We signed up for this.

So---Resistance is futile,
even harmful.

So--
might as well
just go
with the flow.

Live & Let Live

The symphony that prime creator wrote--
is Divine Will.

We all have a part to play
in the Divine Symphony.

There will be an end,
and it will be glorious!

It's gonna get done.

**The Setting Sun**
**by Cheryl**

Every ending
Brings a new beginning,
(Tomorrow is a new day)

A new day
to do something different;
Be different.
Act in a different way.

Think & Be
Calm Yourselves.

A new chance,
Turn the page--
Close the book,
Put it back on the shelf,
and go out and play.

The sun is setting, not long now
before the close of the day--
So, take advantage of the time left,
and make the most of your stay.

# Caledonia is Calling : Alba is Answering
## by Rune Darling

I Don't Know If You See The Changes
That Have Come Over This World
.
These Last Few Years I've Been Wondering If
We Drift Away In Indifference And Materialism
Let's Start Remembering The Old Stories and Ways
Remember Who You Are and Where You Come From
.
I Sense You Through Time
I Am Calling You and In
The Power of The Now
We Are Coming Home
.
Let Me Tell You That You Are Loved
We Are The Children of The Sun and
We Shall Shine Bright Like A Diamond
On The Bonnie Banks of Loch Lomond
.
Some of Us Will Take The High Road
Others Will Take The Low Road
So It Seems That We Have Parted
But We Will All Get There -- In Our Own Time
.
On The Steep Side of Ben Lomond
In a Purple Hue The Highland Anchor is Revealed
The BlueBirds Shall Sing For The White Heart of Dover
As Sunshine and Water Awaken Humanity
.
Let It Be
With Love
Rune Darling
.

# Our Time Has Come
## by Rune Darling

(Getting Lost In The Mind: Sends Shivers Up Our Spine)

So Close No Matter How Far
With Quantum Entanglement
It Couldn't Be Much More From The Heart
Forever Trusting Who We Are

Lets Stand Our Ground Together
Open Ourselves This Way
Life Is Ours & We Live It Our Way
Be of OpenMind For a Different View

Gotta Leave Your Old Version Behind
Face The Truth And Free You Shall Be
I Tell You In All Honesty
You Are A Multidimensional Being

Do You See Me And Realize That We Are Family?
My Heart Is Like An Open Highway
Its Our Life And Its Now Or Never
Also Realize That We Are Gonna Live Forever
.
Live With Your Eyes Wide Open
Take My Hand And Hold It Tight
Exit Night Now Enters Light
We Are Off To Tír ra nÓg
.
Let Us Cast The Blank Rune
Sense Relief In The Unknowable
As The Dagaz Falls On The Finals Table
We Level Out Light And Darkness
.
Like the Colors Of The Rainbow
We Are One In This Together
As We Expand Our Consciousness
We Will Return To The White Light
.
Weaving Frequencies
of Heart-Felt Intuition

## Trust Love
### by Cheryl

trust love,
she'll show the way

no more confusion, competition, doubt--

At the end of the day,
the only choice
is between love and fear.

The sun will set,
and all is well.

## Many thanks to these contributors:

Tommy Allen
Sabinananda Ananda
Christine O'Brien
A'Marie B. Thomas-Brown
Michael Calder
Patricia Carreras
Mikaela Cordeo
Rune Darling
Roger Grossman
Jennifer H.
Dave Harvey
Darrel Johannes
David Kolden
Maria Lodes
Shima Moore
Rene Moraida
Pradeep Nawarathna (pcnawarathna@gmail.com)
Mikasa Tamara Blue Ray
Cody Ray Richardson
Ged Riverstone
Shambala
Shivrael
Mercy Talley
Yvonne Trafton
Winterhawk
Le'Vell Zimmerman

Author page--

Cheryl Lunar Wind lives in the Mount Shasta area in a little town called Weed. She is a practicer of Mayan cosmology, Lakota ceremony, Star Knowledge and the Universal Laws including the Law of One. Her hobbies are writing poetry, music, dance, drum circles and love for all life; plant, animal and crystal. Cheryl has been a guide and spiritual teacher for many years. Now she shares wit and wisdom through poetry, and has published poetry books; Know Your Way, We Are One, Follow the White Rabbit, Love Your Light, LIFE: Shared thru Poetry, Come to Mount Shasta: Sacred Path Poetry, We Are Light, Finding Our Way Home, We Are Forever, Handshake With the Divine, Grand Rising: A New Day Has Dawned, Star Messages: Codes to Sing, Dance and Live by, Return to Innocence, Bloom Like Nature: Live the Natural Way, Creativity Brings Peace: Create & Share Your Gifts, May Love Lead: Poetry for Living, Loving & Giving, The Eventful Flash: Bringing Solar Waves of Change and The Setting Sun.

Testimonials---

"Cheryl's poetry is very inspiring--particularly the way she compares life with the forces of nature. There is a special element in her poems that opens my heart and fills my soul with divine possibilities."
Giovanna Taormina, Co-Founder, One Circle Foundation


"Cheryl's poems have helped me to uncover and honor my own hidden memories. The beauty of her spirit is evident in each tender, insightful passage."
Marguerite Lorimer, www.earthalive.com


"A rare collection filled with raw, courageous honesty. Thought provoking words that will stop you in your tracks."
Snow Thorner, ED Open Sky Gallery, Montague, California

"When wisdom, guidance, confirming comfort, ect. arrives to us humans--from beings with the perspective of other realms--it is a divine gift. Especially in the form of what we call poetry, and through a being with no agenda; Cheryl Lunar Wind simply shares what source gives her!"---Dragon Love (Thomas) Budde


Cheryl,
Greetings and Happy Monday to you my friend. I just wanted to share with you that every time I read 'Come to Mount Shasta', even now that I'm mentioning it I cry, I cannot help it, it is such a Divine message and so impeccable in its timing. I came up here for Spirit, you know I was called by Source and I live on the mountain and I just want to thank you. Your poem found me last summer at the headwaters during the Alien and Angels conference; and then I found your book sitting in the gazebo and I just can't stop, I love it! I love you, thank you.
---Jim


Cheryl,
Just want to thank you for your bringing me into the community at Shasta. What you are doing/did do is absolutely changing my life. You did it, you were instrumental in helping me set my true path. Spirit is moving and the more of us that listen and act the sooner the shift will be completed.
---Darrel


About Cheryl's poetry--
"You are dynamic! I have known no one who does so much so swiftly, and your writing touches my heart because it comes from your heart."
---The Durwood Show


"Your words are my words. I keep your book 'Know Your Way' on my nightstand. I read it at bedtime and morning."
---Karina Arroyo

Made in the USA
Columbia, SC
03 January 2025